Billboard
ADULT CONTEMPORARY HITS

Arranged by Dan Coates

Alfred

Produced by
Alfred Music Publishing Co., Inc.
P.O. Box 10003
Van Nuys, CA 91410-0003
alfred.com

Printed in USA.

ISBN-10: 0-7390-7049-5
ISBN-13: 978-0-7390-7049-9

 Alfred Cares. Contents printed on 100% recycled paper.

AMAZED

Words and Music by
Marv Green, Aimee Mayo and Chris Lindsey
Arranged by Dan Coates

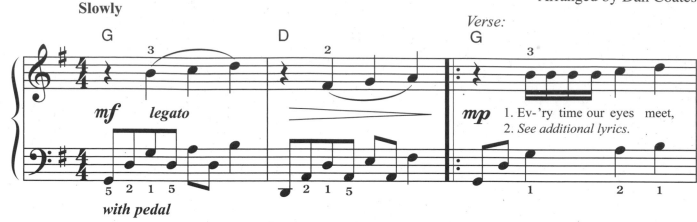

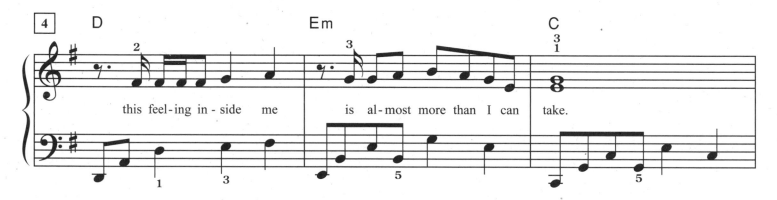

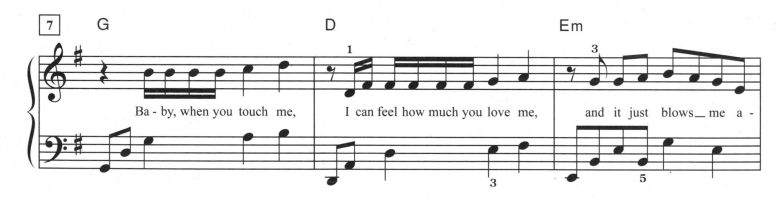

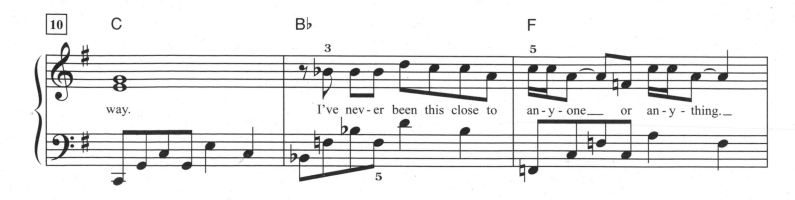

I can hear your thoughts,

I can see your ___ dreams.

Chorus:

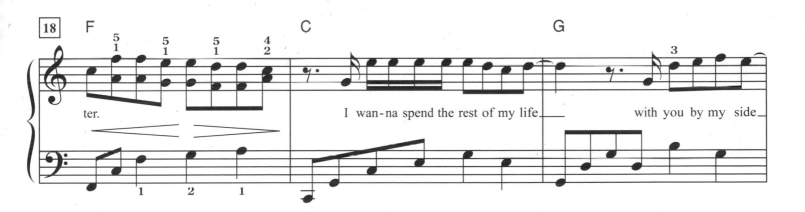

I don't know how you do what you do. ___

I'm so in love with you.

It just keeps get-ting bet-

ter.

I wan-na spend the rest of my life ___

with you by my side ___

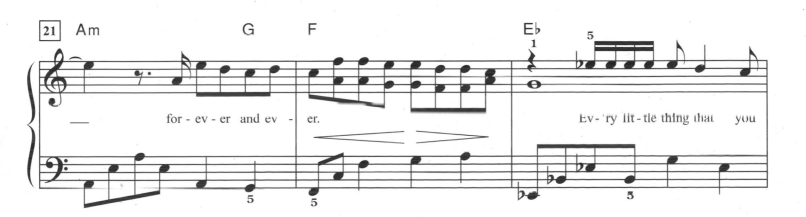

___ for - ev - er and ev - er.

Ev - 'ry lit - tle thing that you

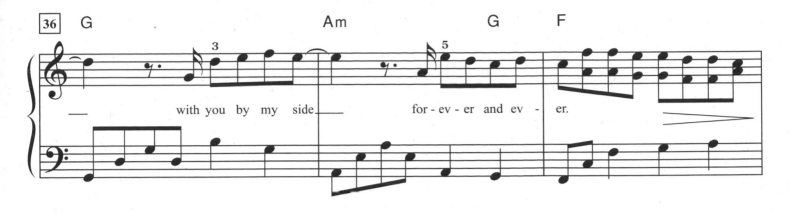

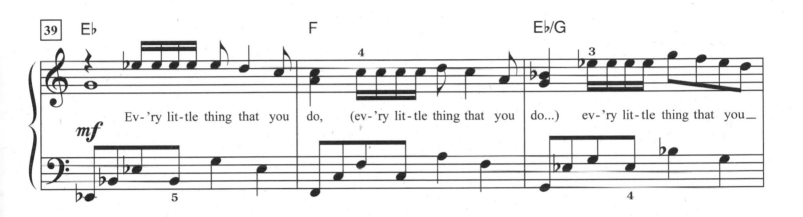

Verse 2:
The smell of your skin,
The taste of your kiss,
The way you whisper in the dark.
Your hair all around me,
Baby, you surround me.
You touch every place in my heart.
Oh, it feels like the first time every time.
I wanna spend the whole night in your eyes.
(To Chorus:)

BECAUSE OF YOU

Words and Music by
Kelly Clarkson, Ben Moody and David Hodges
Arranged by Dan Coates

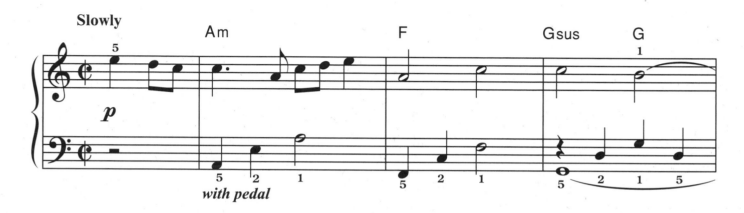

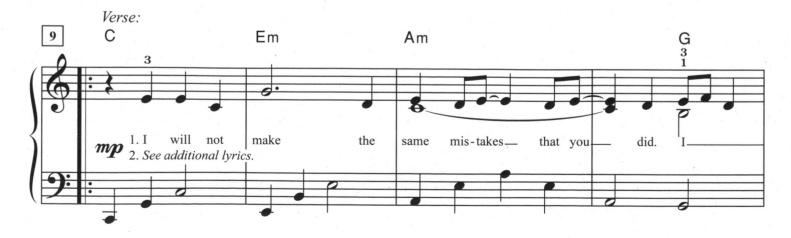

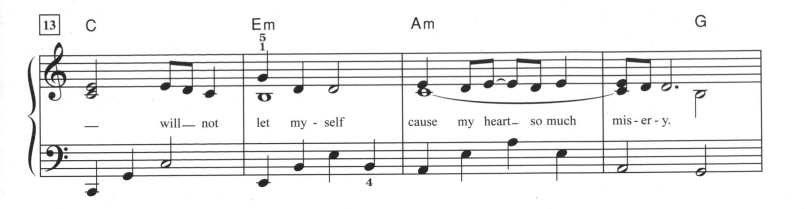

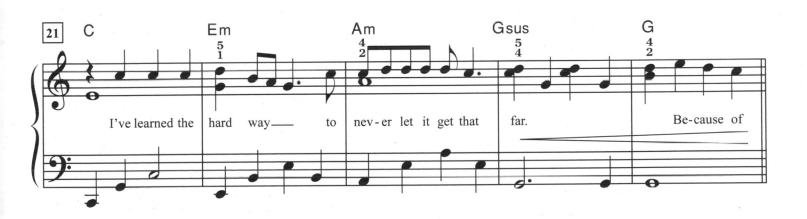

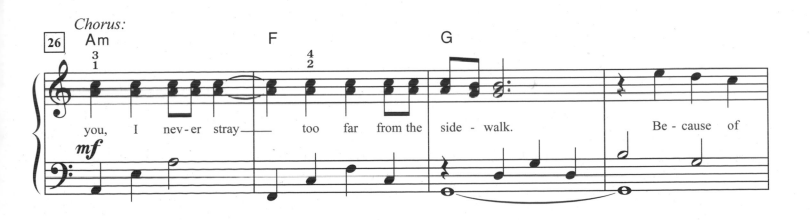

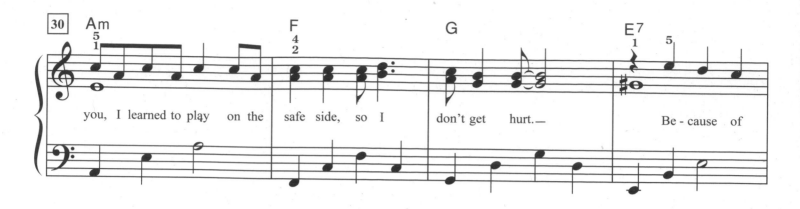

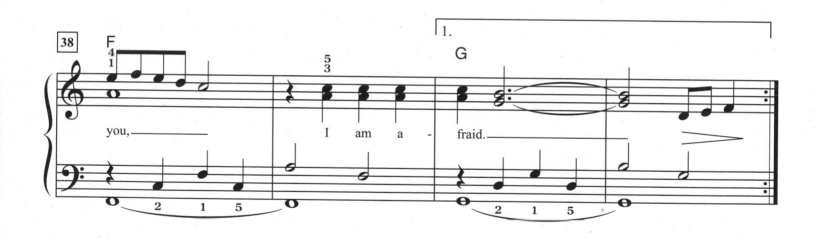

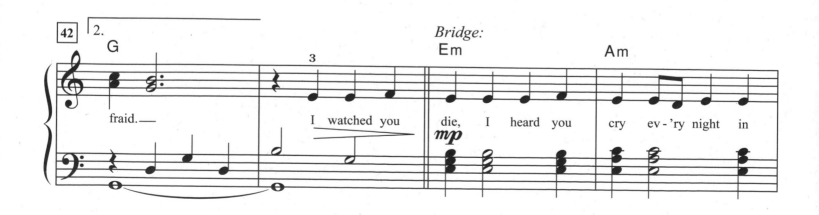

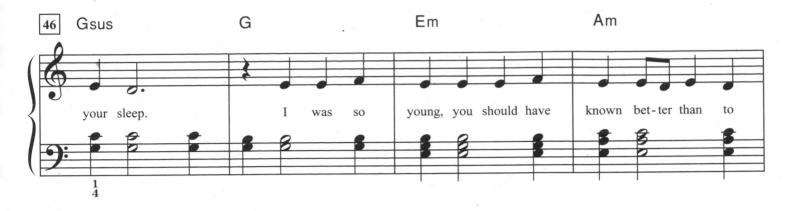

your sleep. I was so young, you should have known bet-ter than to

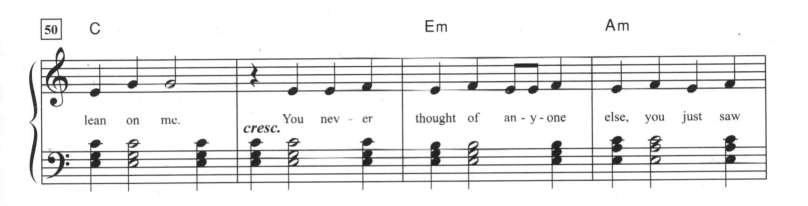

lean on me. *cresc.* You nev - er thought of an - y - one else, you just saw

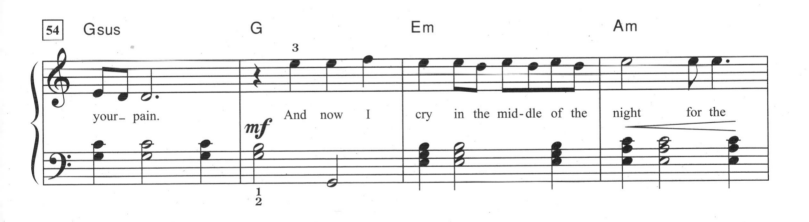

your— pain. *mf* And now I cry in the mid-dle of the night for the

same damn thing. Be - cause of

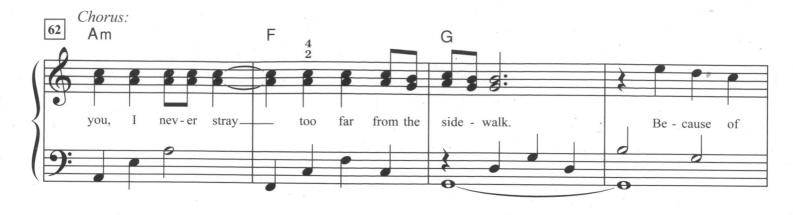

Chorus:

you, I nev-er stray___ too far from the side-walk. Be-cause of

you, I learned to play on the safe side so I don't get hurt.__ *cresc.* Be-cause of

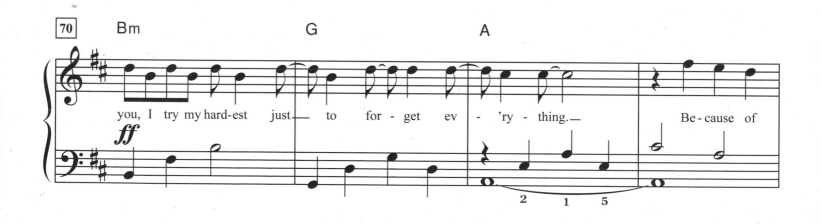

you, I try my hard-est just__ to for-get ev-'ry-thing.__ Be-cause of

you, I don't know how to let__ an-y-one else__ in. Be-cause__ of

Verse 2:
I lose my way,
And it's not too long before you point it out.
I cannot cry,
Because I know that's weakness in your eyes.
I'm forced to fake a smile,
A laugh, every day of my life.
My heart can't possibly break
When it wasn't even whole to start with.
(To Chorus:)

BREAKAWAY

Words and Music by
Matthew Gerrard, Bridget Benenate and Avril Lavigne
Arranged by Dan Coates

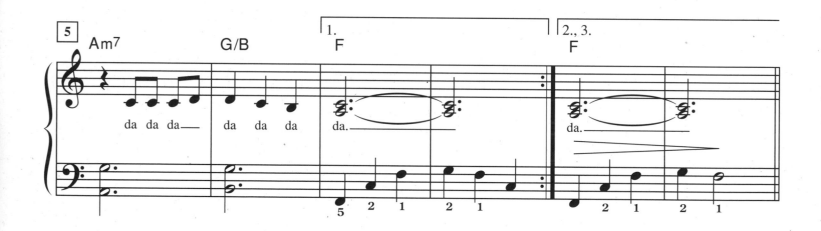

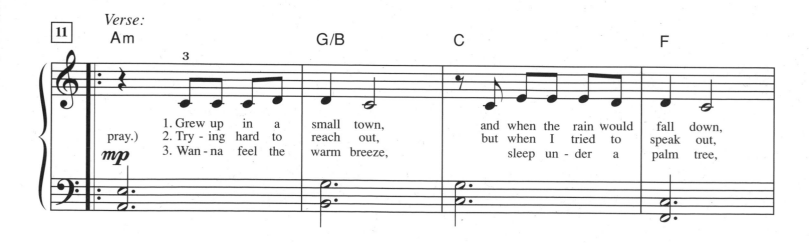

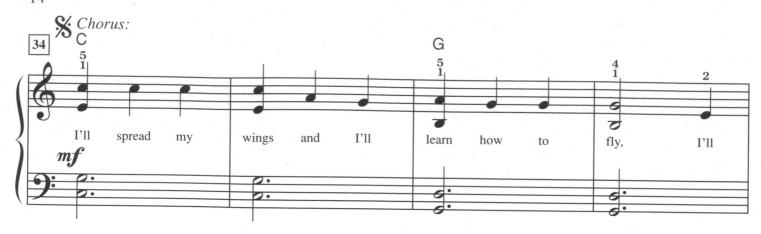

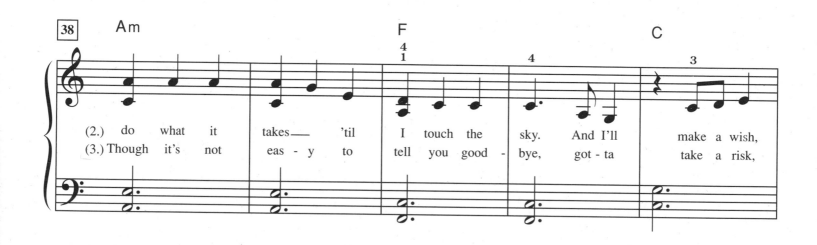

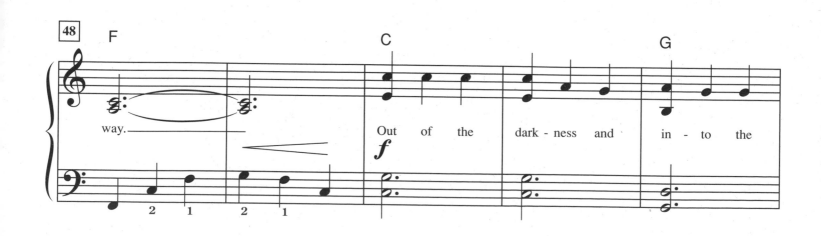

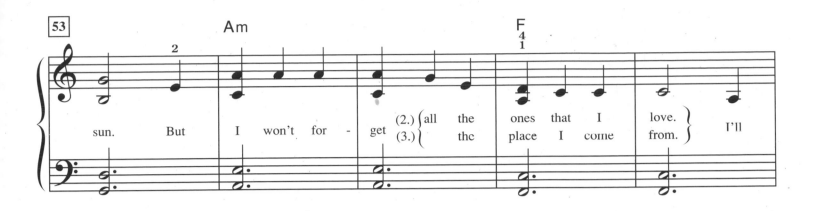

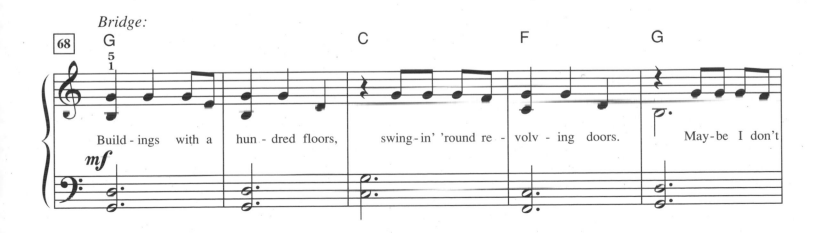

15

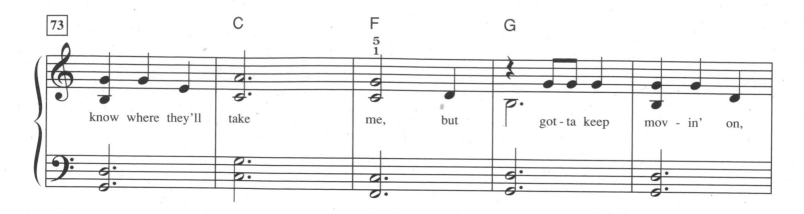

know where they'll take me, but got - ta keep mov - in' on,

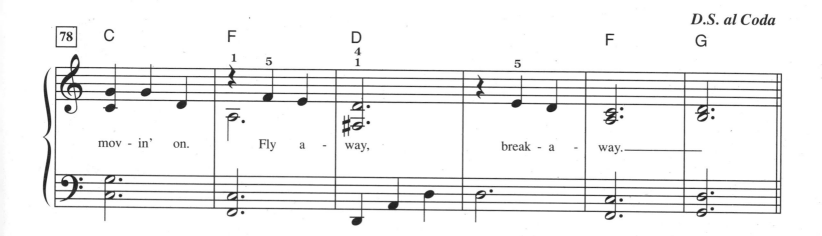

D.S. al Coda

mov - in' on. Fly a - way, break - a - way.

Coda

break - a - way, break -

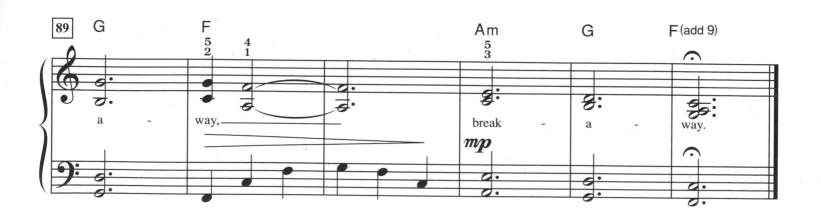

a - way, break - a - way.

mp

THE GAME OF LOVE

Words and Music by
Gregg Alexander and Rick Nowells
Arranged by Dan Coates

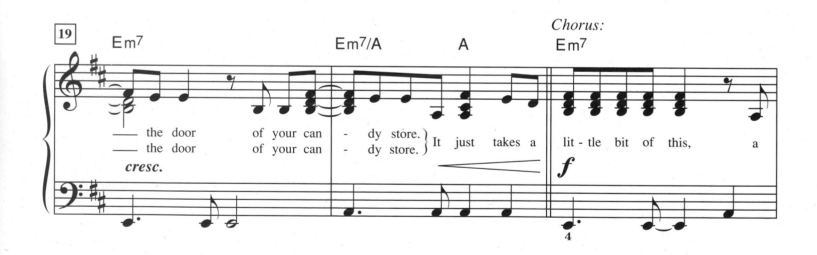

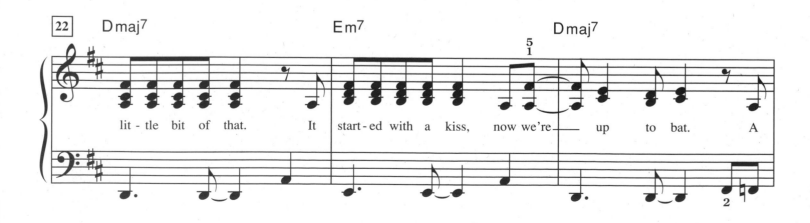

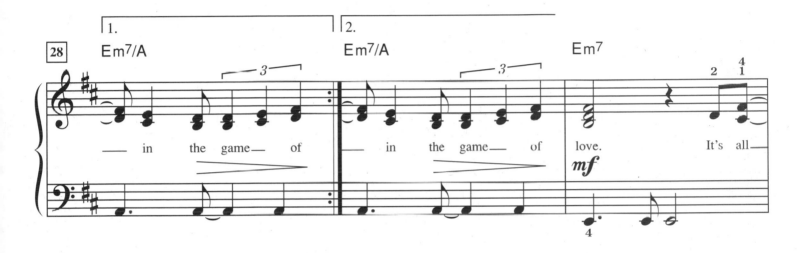

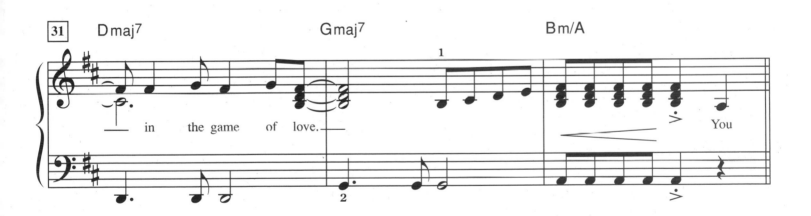

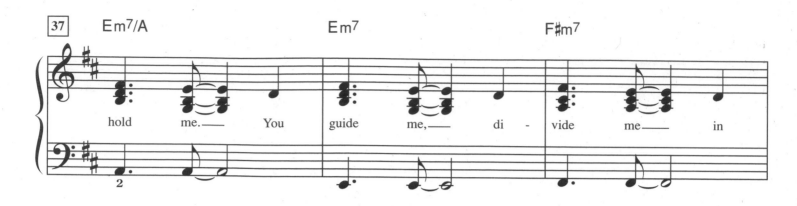

hold me.— You guide me,— di - vide me— in

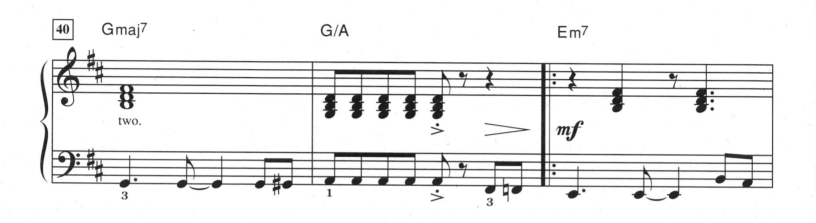

two.

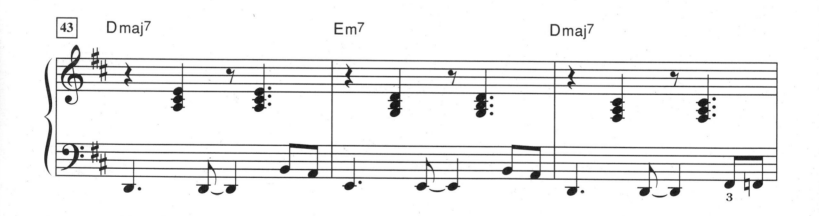

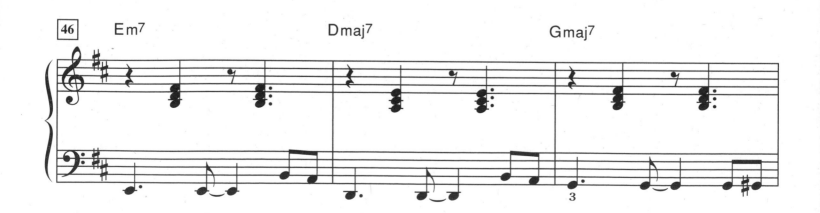

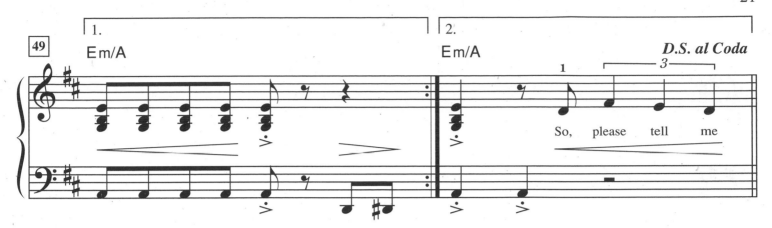

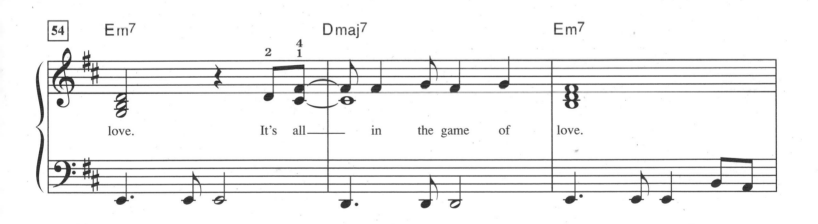

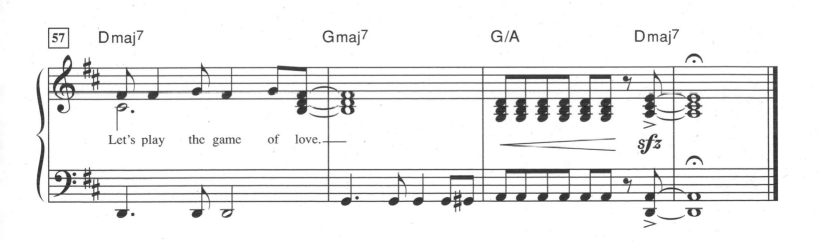

EVERYTHING

Words and Music by
Michael Bublé, Alan Chang and Amy Foster
Arranged by Dan Coates

Moderately, with a steady beat

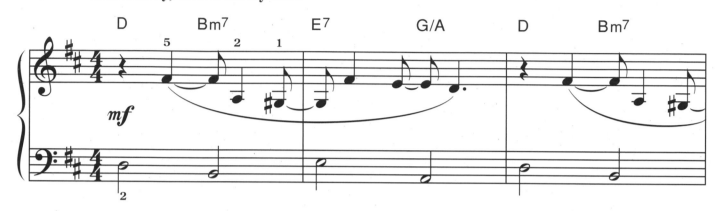

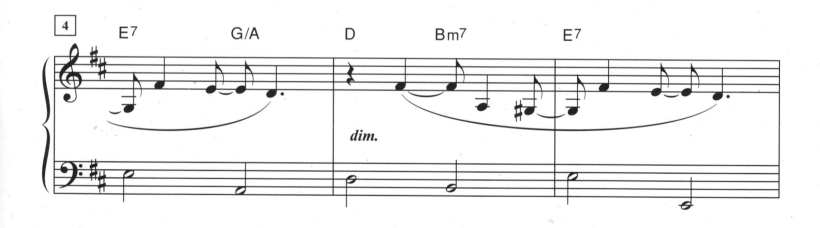

1. You're a fall - ing star, you're the get -
ou - sel, you're a wish -

HEY THERE DELILAH

Words and Music by Tom Higgenson
Arranged by Dan Coates

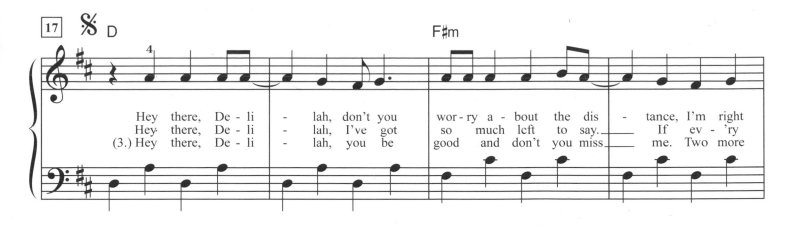

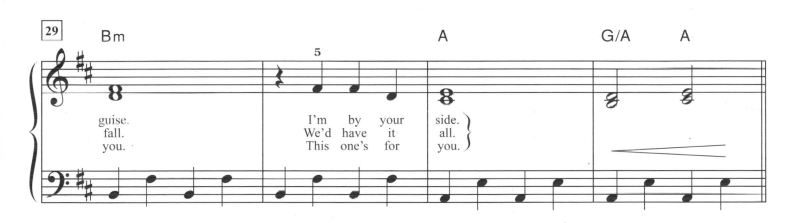

HOME

Words and Music by
Michael Bublé, Alan Chang And Amy Foster
Arranged by Dan Coates

Moderately slow

Verse:

An - oth - er sum - mer day has come and gone a - way

mp

with pedal

in Par - is and Rome, but I wan - na go home.

May be sur - round - ed by a mil - lion peo - ple; I still feel all a - lone,

I HOPE YOU DANCE

By Mark D. Sanders and Tia Sillers
Arranged by Dan Coates

Verse:

hope you nev-er lose your sense of won-der. You get your
2. *See additional lyrics.*

fill to eat, but al-ways keep that hun-ger. May you

nev-er take one sin-gle breath for grant-ed. God for-

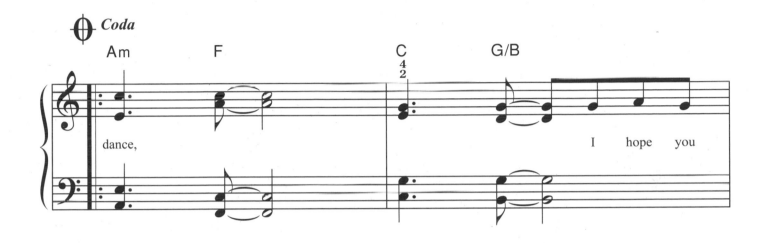

Verse 2:
I hope you never fear those mountains in the distance,
Never settle for the path of least resistance.
Livin' might mean takin' chances but they're worth takin'.
Lovin' might be a mistake but it's worth makin'.
(To Chorus:)

Verse 3:
Don't let some hell-bent heart leave you bitter.
When you come close to sellin' out, reconsider.
Give the heavens above more than just a passing glance.
And when you get the choice to sit it out or dance,
I hope you dance.
(To Chorus:)

I KNEW I LOVED YOU

Words and Music by
Daniel Jones and Darren Hayes
Arranged by Dan Coates

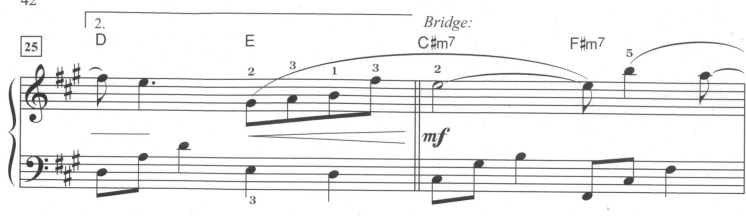

Bridge:

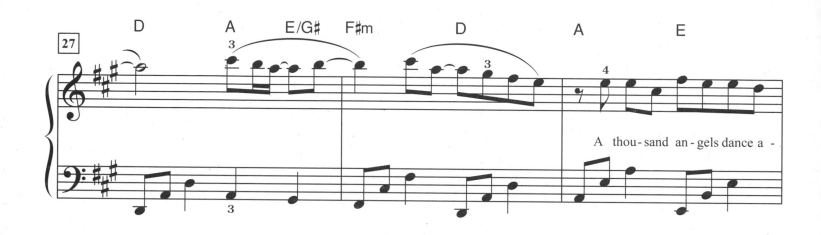

A thou-sand an-gels dance a-

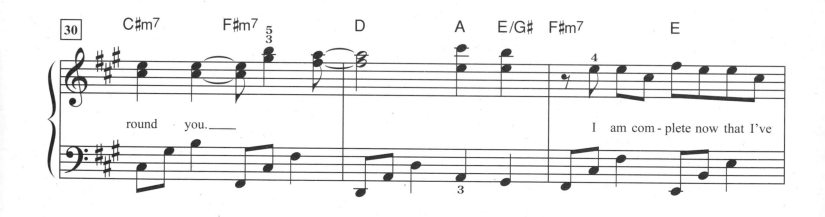

round you.___ I am com-plete now that I've

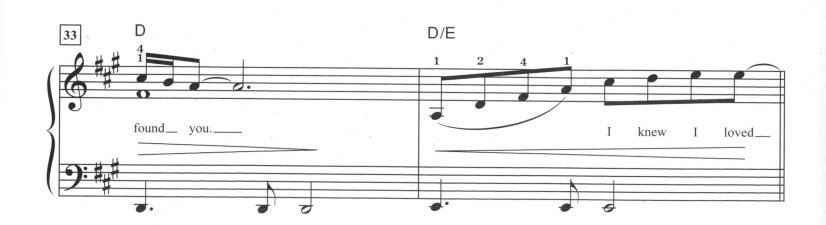

found__ you.___ I knew I loved__

I TURN TO YOU

Words and Music by Diane Warren
Arranged by Dan Coates

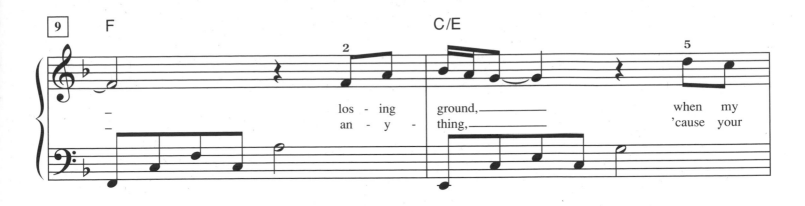

46

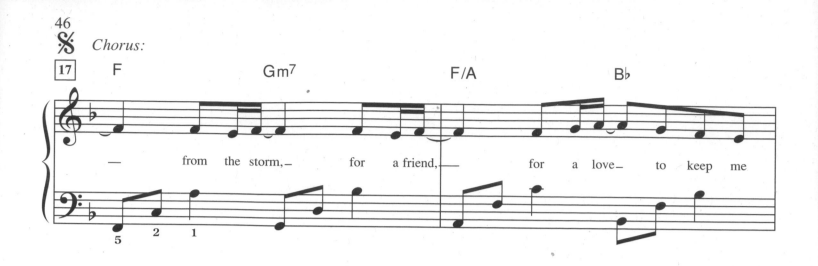

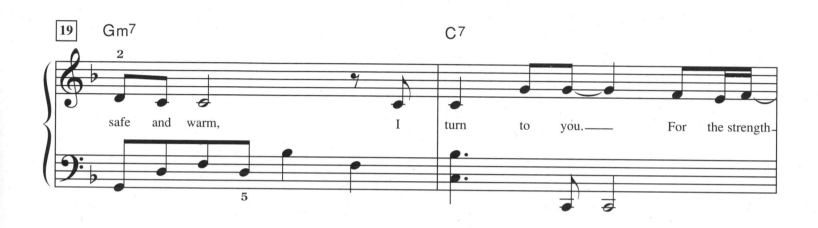

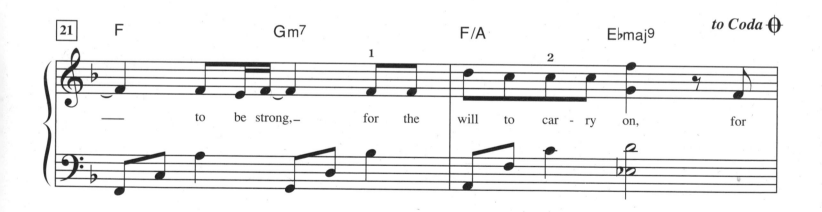

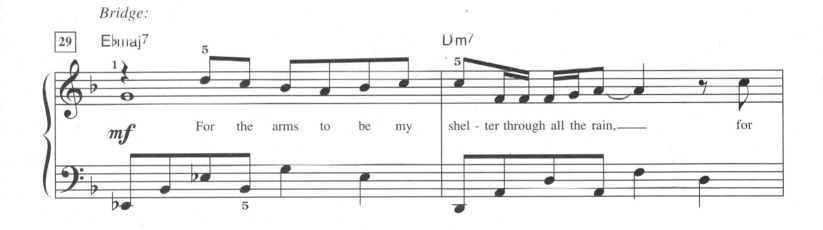

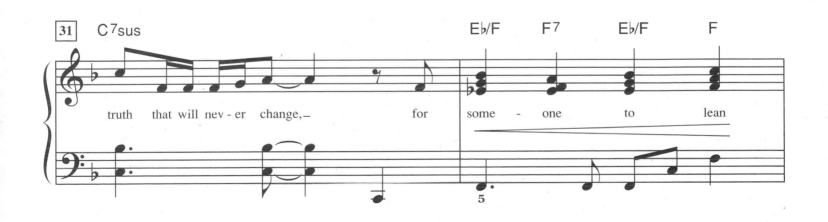

33 Eb ... Bb/D

on, for a heart I can re - ly on through an-y-thing,___ for that

35 Gm7/C ... C7 ... *D.S. al Coda*

one who___ I can run to. For a shield___

Coda
Gm7 ... Db/Eb ... C7sus

ev - 'ry-thing— you do, for ev - 'ry-thing— that's true, for

39 Gm7 ... Db/Eb ... C7sus ... F

ev - 'ry-thing— you do, for ev - 'ry-thing— that's true, I turn to you.

molto rit.

LIVE LIKE YOU WERE DYING

Words and Music by
Tim Nichols and Craig Wiseman
Arranged by Dan Coates

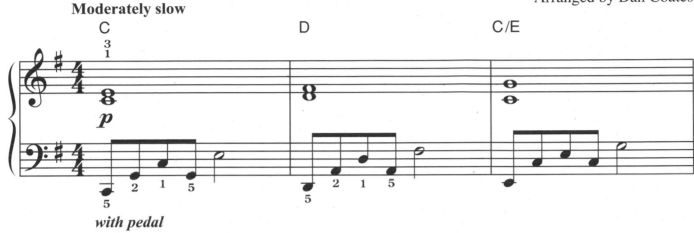

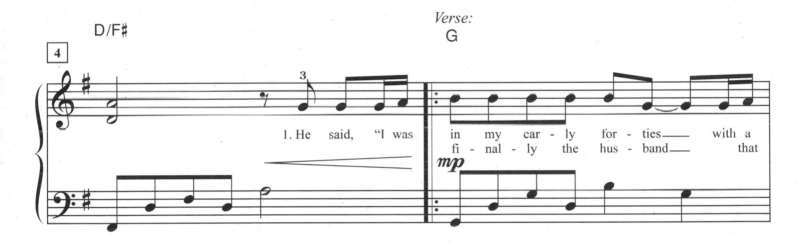

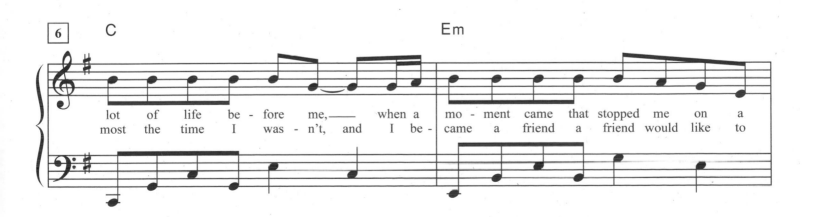

50

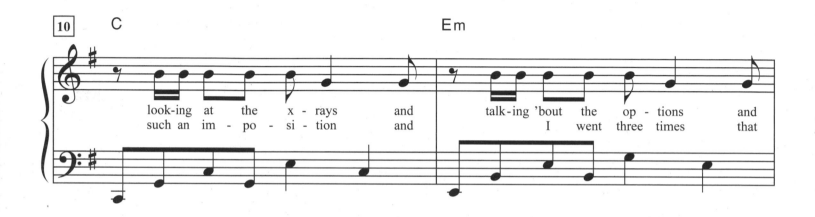

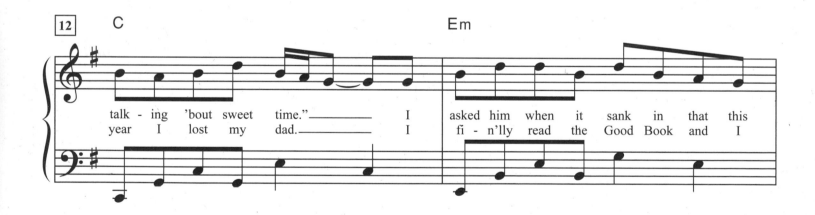

Chorus:

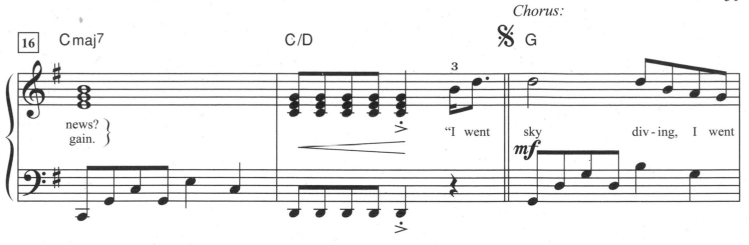

16 Cmaj7   C/D   %. G

news? / gain.   *mf* "I went sky div - ing, I went

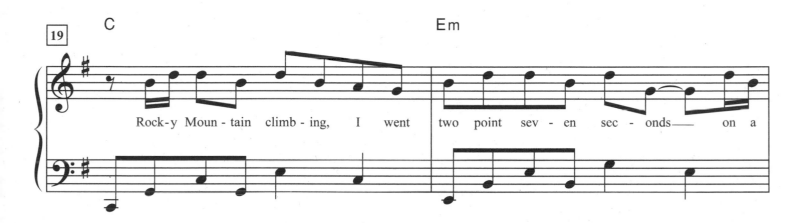

19 C   Em

Rock-y Moun - tain climb - ing, I went two point sev - en sec - onds —— on a

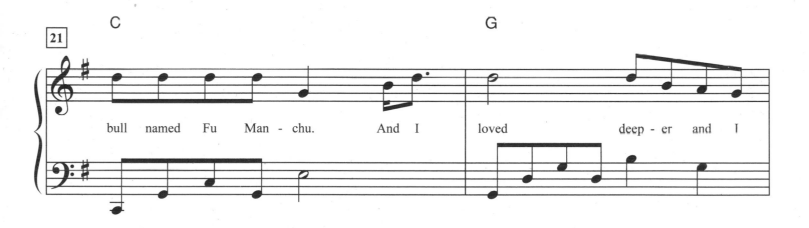

21 C   G

bull named Fu Man - chu. And I loved deep - er and I

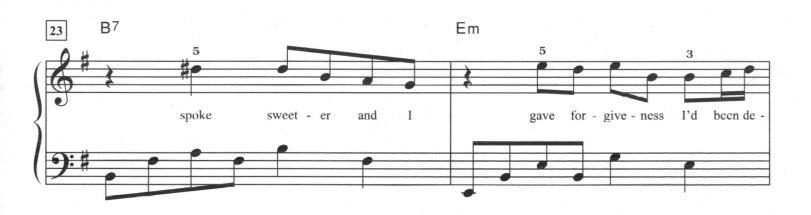

23 B7   Em

spoke sweet - er and I gave for - give - ness I'd bccn de -

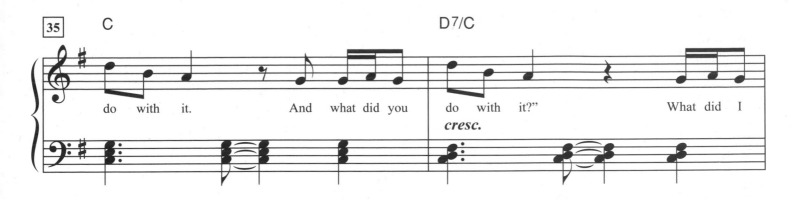

LOST

Words and Music by
Michael Bublé, Alan Chang and Jann Arden
Arranged by Dan Coates

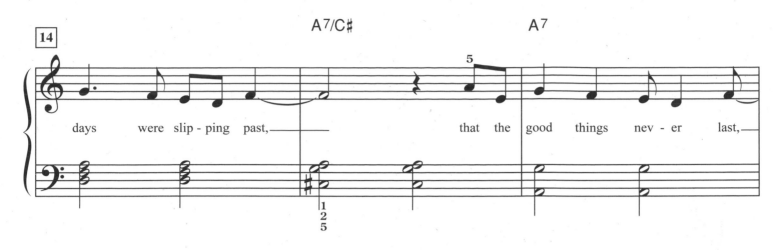

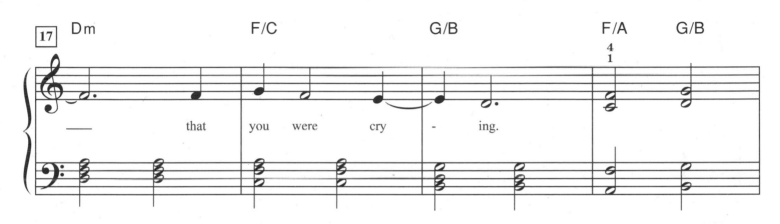

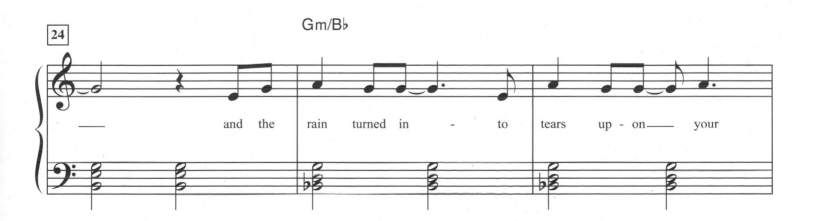

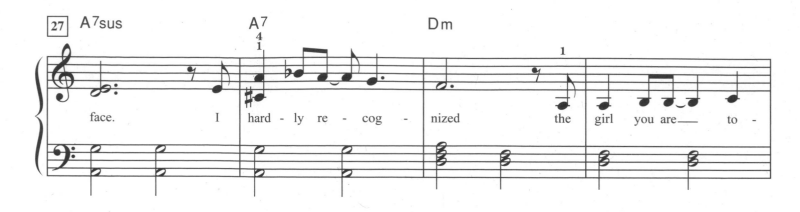

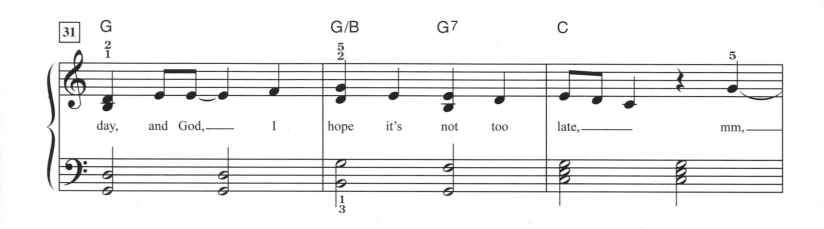

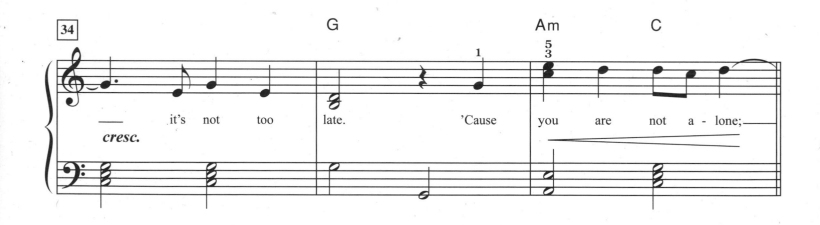

Chorus:

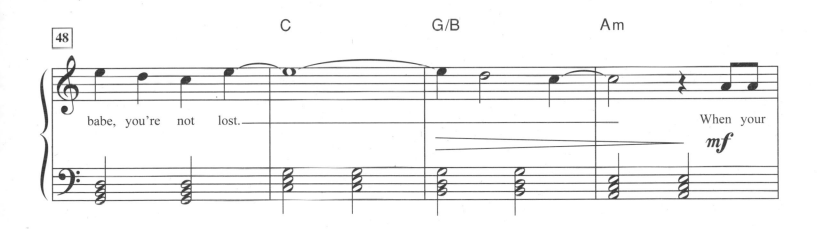

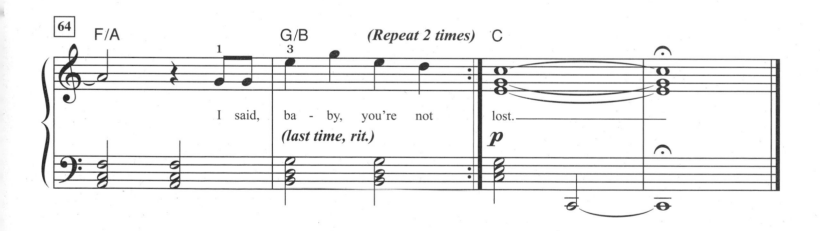

Verse 3:
Life can show no mercy;
It can tear your soul apart.
It can make you feel like you've gone crazy
But you're not.
Though things have seemed to change,
There's one thing that's the same.
In my heart you have remained
And we can fly, fly, fly away.
(To Chorus:)

SHOW ME THE MEANING OF BEING LONELY

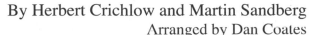

By Herbert Crichlow and Martin Sandberg
Arranged by Dan Coates

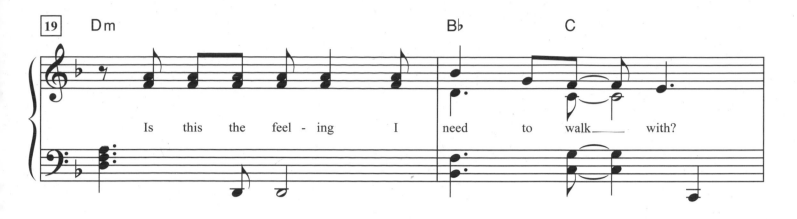

Is this the feel - ing I need to walk____ with?

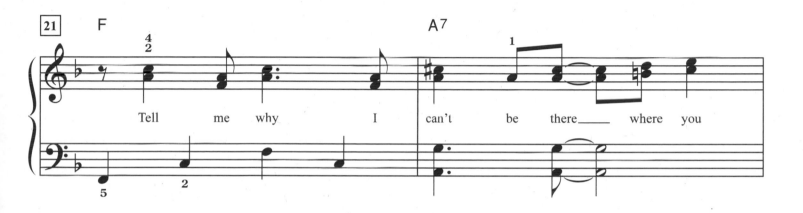

Tell me why I can't be there____ where you

are? There's some-thing miss-ing in my heart.

some - thing miss - ing in my

Is this the feel - ing I need to walk____ with?

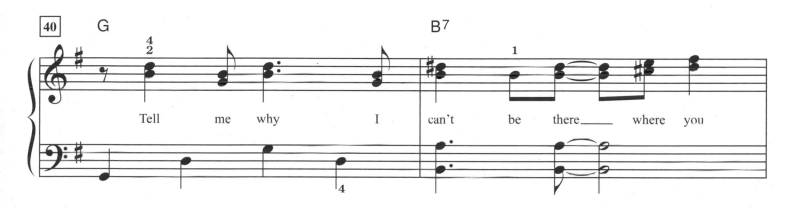

Tell me why I can't be there____ where you

are? There's some - thing miss - ing in my heart.

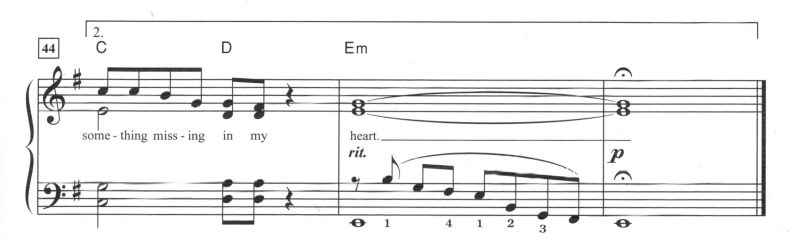

some - thing miss - ing in my heart.____

THAT'S THE WAY IT IS

Words and Music by
Max Martin, Kristian Lundin and Andreas Carlsson
Arranged by Dan Coates

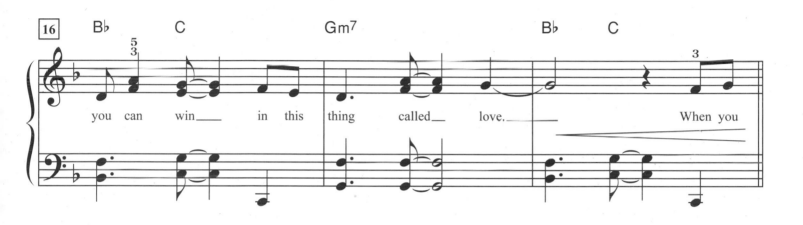

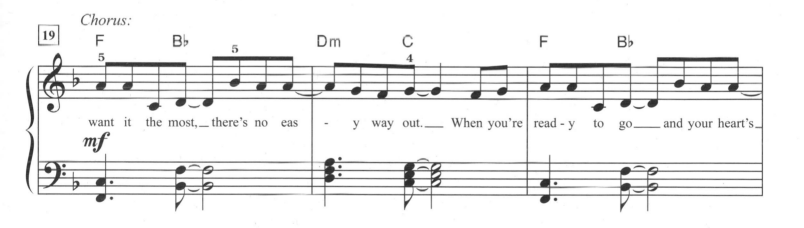

THERE YOU'LL BE

Words and Music by Diane Warren
Arranged by Dan Coates

Chorus:

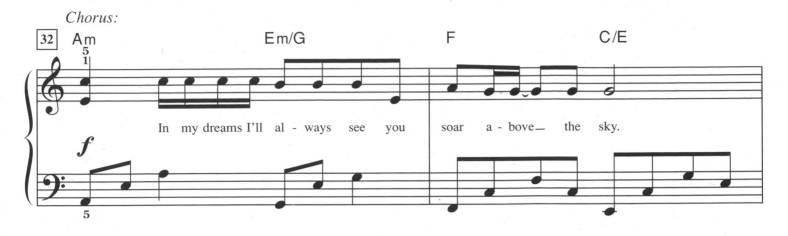

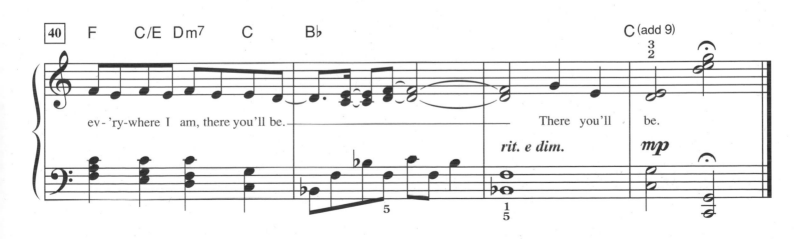

THANK YOU

Words and Music by
Dido Armstrong and Paul Herman
Arranged by Dan Coates

1. My tea's gone cold, I'm won-d'ring why I_____ got out of bed at
2. *See additional lyrics.*

all. The morn-ing rain clouds up my win-dow and I can't see at

all. And e-ven if I could, it-'d all be gray, but your pic-ture on my

Verse 2:
I drank too much last night, got bills to pay,
My head just feels in pain.
I missed the bus and there'll be hell today,
I'm late for work again.
And even if I'm there, they'll all imply
That I might not last the day.
And then you call me and it's not so bad, it's not so bad.
(To Chorus:)

THIS I PROMISE YOU

Words and Music by Richard Marx
Arranged by Dan Coates

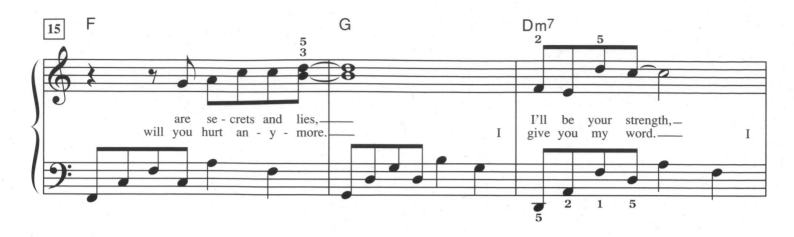

15 F · · · · · · · G · · · · · · · Dm7

are se-crets and lies, — I'll be your strength, — I
will you hurt an-y-more. — give you my word. —

18 G7 · · · · · · · C · · G/B · · · Am

I'll give you hope, — keep-ing your faith — when it's gone. — The
give you my heart. — This is a bat - tle we've won. — And

21 Dm7 · · · · · · · Fm · · · · · · · Gsus

one you should call — was stand-ing here all — a - long. —
with — this vow, — for - ev - er has now — be - gun. —

Chorus:

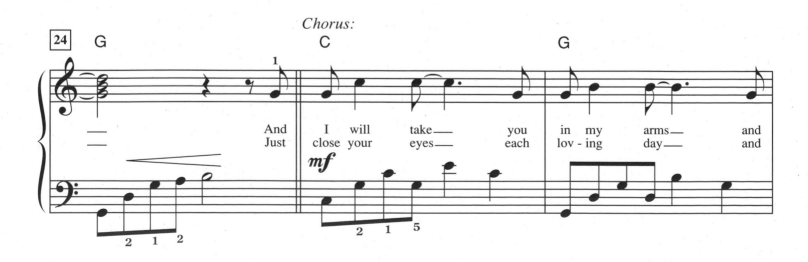

24 G · · · · · · · C · · · · · · · G

— And I will take — you in my arms — and
— Just close your eyes — each lov - ing day — and

mf

With-out you ___ in my life, ___ ba - by, I just

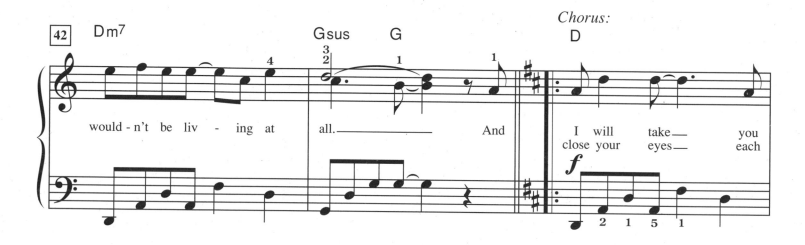

would-n't be liv - ing at all. ___ And

Chorus:

I will take ___ you
close your eyes ___ each

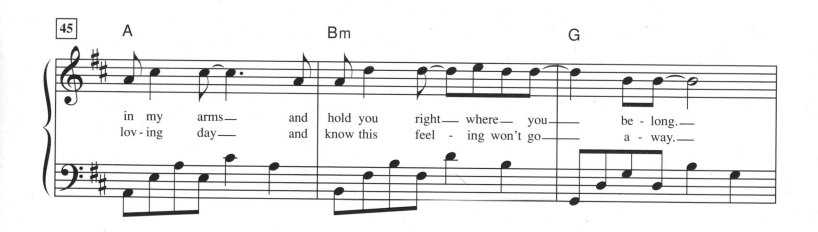

in my arms ___ and hold you right ___ where ___ you ___ be - long. ___
lov - ing day ___ and know this feel - ing won't go ___ a - way. ___

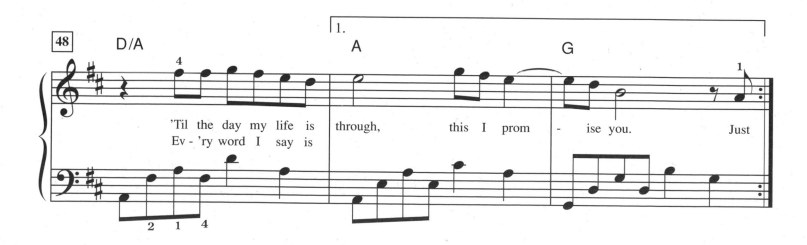

1.

'Til the day my life is through, this I prom - ise you. Just
Ev - 'ry word I say is

true, this I prom - ise you.

Ev - 'ry word I say is true, this I prom - ise you.

mf

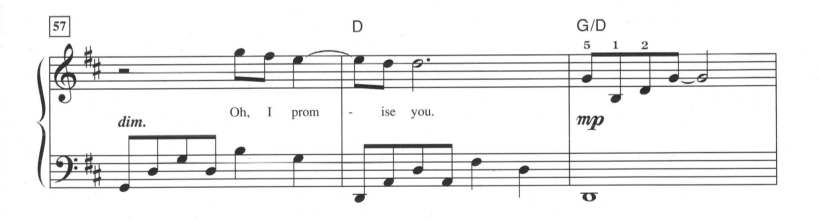

dim. Oh, I prom - ise you. *mp*

rit. *p*

TO WHERE YOU ARE

Words and Music by
Richard Marx and Linda Thompson
Arranged by Dan Coates

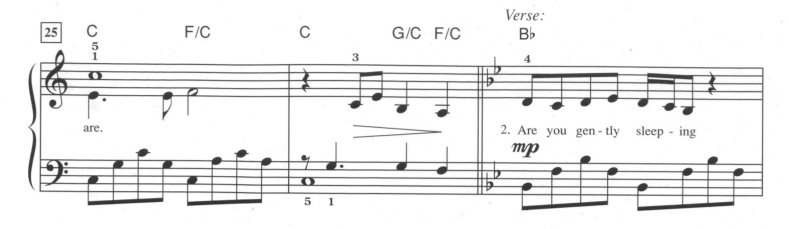

Verse:

are.

2. Are you gen-tly sleep-ing

here in-side my dream? And is-n't faith be-liev-ing all pow-er can't— be seen?

As my heart holds— you just one beat a-way, I cher-ish all you gave me ev-'ry

cresc.

Chorus:

day.————————— 'Cause you are my for-ev-er love watch-ing

WHITE FLAG

Words and Music by
Dido Armstrong, Richard Nowels and Rollo Armstrong
Arranged by Dan Coates

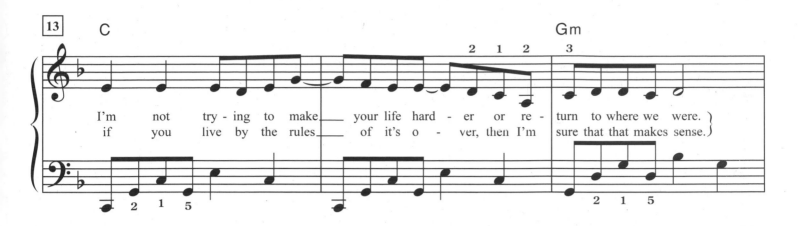

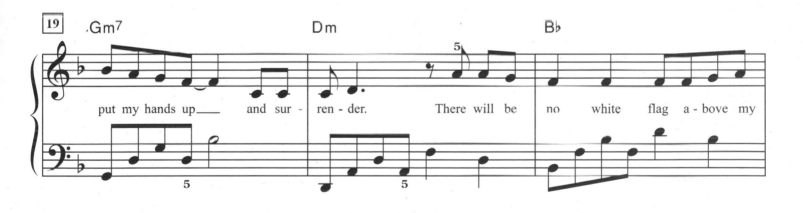

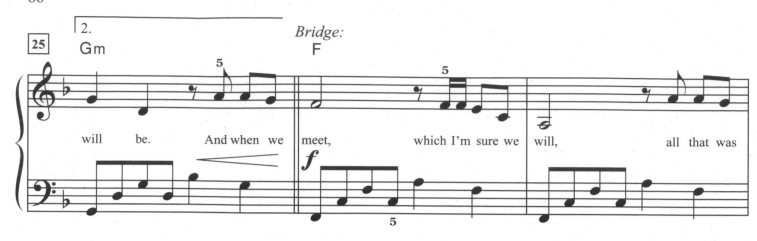

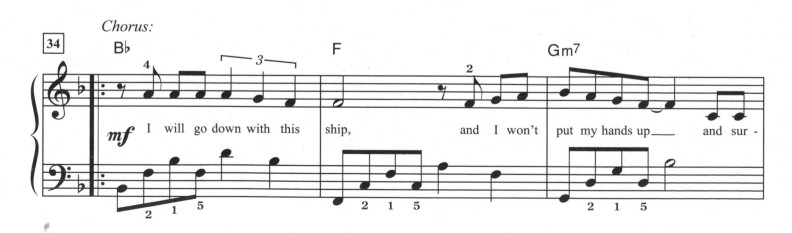

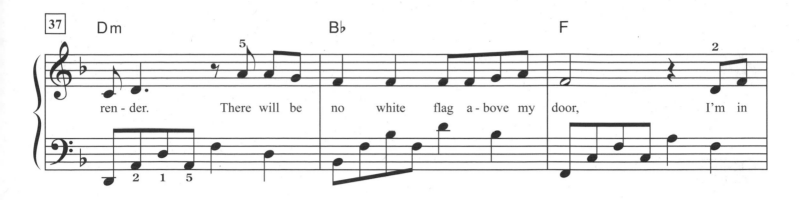

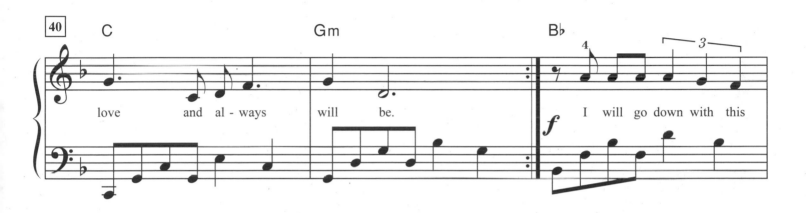

YOU AND ME

Words and Music by
Jason Wade and Jude Cole
Arranged by Dan Coates

Moderately slow

Verse:

Lyrics:
1. What day is it, and in what month? This
2. All of the things that I want to say

clock nev-er seemed so a-live.
just aren't com-ing out right. I'm

I can't keep up, and I can't back down. I've been
trip-ping on words. You got my head spin-ning. I

los-ing so much time.
can't know where to go from here.

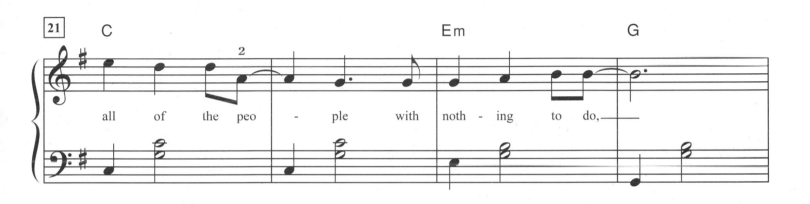

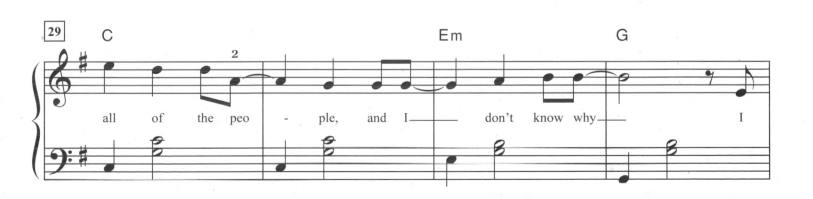